Original title:
The Power of Love

Copyright © 2024 Swan Charm
All rights reserved.

Author: Olivia Orav
ISBN HARDBACK: 978-9916-89-631-0
ISBN PAPERBACK: 978-9916-89-632-7
ISBN EBOOK: 978-9916-89-633-4

Transcendent Unity

In a dance of light and shade,
We find the threads that weave our fate.
Each heartbeat sings a silent tune,
In night's embrace, we feel the moon.

Upon the whisper of the breeze,
The echoes of our dreams release.
Together, hands entwined, we soar,
United souls, forevermore.

The cosmos hums a gentle song,
In its rhythm, we belong.
With every star that lights the sky,
A spark of love, we can't deny.

Through the valleys, through the heights,
We walk in peace, beneath the lights.
In every glance, we understand,
A bond that time cannot withstand.

In every heart, a universe,
In every step, we feel the verse.
Although apart, we're never lone,
In transcendent unity, we've grown.

Hearth of Memories

A crackling fire, soft and bright,
Illuminates the fallen night.
Each flicker tells a tale of old,
In warmth and whispers, dreams unfold.

Photos hang on weathered walls,
Echoes of laughter in the halls.
Moments captured, time retains,
In every corner, love remains.

The scent of spice, the sound of cheer,
A gathering of loved ones near.
Stories shared beneath the glow,
The hearth of memories starts to flow.

With every mug raised to the sky,
Reminders that we're not alone,
Through seasons lost, we find our way,
In comfort's clasp, we choose to stay.

Time moves on, yet here we stand,
A circle formed, hand in hand.
In this embrace, we find our rest,
The hearth of memories, truly blessed.

Mosaic of Memories

Fragments of laughter, moments we shared,
Colors of joy in the memories declared.
Each piece a tale, a story untold,
Together we weave a tapestry bold.

Faded photographs, a whisper of time,
Echoes of love in each heartbeat's chime.
In shadows and sunlight, our lives intertwine,
A mosaic of memories, forever we'll shine.

Celestial Union

Stars gently flicker in the night so bright,
Guiding our hearts with their shimmering light.
In the vast sky, our dreams take flight,
A celestial union, a bond of delight.

Galaxies dance in a cosmic embrace,
Time stands still in this boundless space.
Together we wander, lost in the grace,
Finding our rhythm in love's warm trace.

Canvas of Togetherness

Brush strokes of kindness paint our delight,
On this canvas, our spirits ignite.
Hues of compassion blend and they twine,
Creating a masterpiece, yours and mine.

Each moment a color, vibrant and true,
Splashing the world with the love that we drew.
In this gallery of life, I see the view,
A canvas of togetherness, bright and anew.

Heartstrings Entwined

Tugging gently on the strands of our fate,
Threads of affection that sustain and elate.
In harmony, woven, our spirits align,
Creating a symphony, heartstrings entwined.

Resonating softly, the melody flows,
Binding our souls as each heartbeat knows.
Together we'll dance, as the universe shows,
In this sweet serenade, love only grows.

Love's Resilient Echo

In shadows deep, love finds its way,
Through whispered dreams, a bright bouquet.
With every scar, a story grows,
In tender hearts, true passion glows.

Through storms and trials, we hold on tight,
In darkest hours, we seek the light.
The echo lingers, strong yet sweet,
A symphony where two hearts meet.

Time may bend, but never break,
In every choice, love is awake.
With steadfast hope, we rise above,
A timeless dance, this gift of love.

Enchanting Alchemy

In moonlit nights, dreams take their flight,
Whispers of magic, pure delight.
Transforming hearts with each gentle touch,
The alchemy of love means so much.

Through laughter bright, and silent sighs,
In every glance, a new surprise.
Moments weave a mystic thread,
A tapestry where souls are led.

Crimson blossoms, the scent of spring,
In every heartbeat, love takes wing.
Merging worlds in radiant hues,
Grand symphonies with softest blues.

Hidden Gardens of Emotion

In secret nooks where feelings bloom,
Quiet spaces, dispelling gloom.
Petals of joy, thorns of despair,
Tender roots bind, a love so rare.

Through tangled vines and morning dew,
Hidden gardens reveal what's true.
Soft murmurs breeze through ancient trees,
A dance of hearts upon the seas.

In shadows cast, the light will find,
Whispers of hope, the soul entwined.
Growth in silence, the fragrance sweet,
In these gardens, we are complete.

The Rapture of Belonging

In arms embraced, our spirits soar,
A sanctuary where hearts explore.
The rapture sings in every tie,
A bond that lifts us toward the sky.

In laughter shared, in tears we shed,
Through open doors, love's path we tread.
Together we chase the setting sun,
In every heartbeat, we are one.

With gentle grace, we find our place,
In woven threads, a sacred space.
In unity, our souls belong,
In the rapture of love's sweet song.

Flames of Purpose

In the heart where passion burns,
Each ember whispers, life returns.
Through trials faced, we rise anew,
With purpose bold, we'll see it through.

The winds may wail, the shadows creep,
Yet in our souls, the fire we keep.
With every step, we forge our way,
In unity, we'll greet the day.

We chase the sparks, ignite our dreams,
In every hardship, hope redeems.
Together strong, we face the night,
With flames of purpose, we'll find light.

Let courage reign, let fears subside,
With open hearts, we will not hide.
We'll fan the flames, let spirits soar,
In every breath, we'll ask for more.

As wisdom grows and journeys blend,
The fire within will never end.
In shared endeavors, we will stand,
With flames of purpose, hand in hand.

Paths of Connection

Along the trails where footsteps meet,
Each shared moment, a heartbeat.
As stories weave and laughter flows,
In bonds of love, our spirit grows.

Through winding roads and whispered dreams,
The thread of life in sunlight gleams.
Unseen ties bind us, heart to heart,
In every journey, we play our part.

In silence shared, in glances bright,
We find our way through day and night.
Together, we embrace the call,
In paths of connection, we stand tall.

When storms arise, we seek the calm,
With open arms, we share the balm.
In unity, our strength will show,
On paths of connection, love will grow.

With every step, our stories blend,
In joy and sorrow, we transcend.
Together, we shall light the way,
On paths of connection, come what may.

Garden of Dreams

In a garden lush, where hopes take flight,
Every blossom glimmers bright.
With whispered wishes in the air,
We plant our dreams with tender care.

Beneath the sun and gentle rain,
We cultivate both joy and pain.
With roots entwined, we thrive and grow,
In a garden where our spirits glow.

Each fragrance sweet, each color bright,
A tapestry of pure delight.
In every petal, a promise waits,
In the garden of dreams, love resonates.

As seasons change, we learn to trust,
In every storm, it's love that's just.
Together we'll face the unknown,
In our garden of dreams, we're not alone.

As twilight falls, the stars align,
In this haven, hearts entwine.
In every flower, a story gleams,
In the quiet night of the garden of dreams.

Refuge in Each Other

In the storm's embrace, we seek retreat,
With open arms, our hearts will meet.
Through trials faced, side by side,
In moments shared, we will abide.

When shadows loom and darkness calls,
With whispered hope, love gently falls.
In your gaze, I find my peace,
A refuge strong, where fears release.

In laughter's glow and tearful sighs,
Together we rise, beneath vast skies.
In every heartbeat, a gentle tether,
In the warmth of love, we'll weather.

Through thick and thin, our spirits blend,
In trust we build, a love to tend.
With you, I find my strength and grace,
In refuge in each other, a sacred space.

As days turn bright and seasons wane,
In our embrace, we shed the pain.
For in this life, come what may,
We'll be each other's light, our way.

The Star-Crossed Journey

Beneath the night's vast, endless dome,
Two souls emerged, far from their home.
With whispered dreams and hearts ablaze,
They chased the dawn through tangled maze.

Paths intertwined like vines of gold,
Yet fate, it seems, is always bold.
As shadows danced and stars did sigh,
They forged ahead, refusing to die.

Lighthouses in the Storm

When tempests roar and waters rise,
A beacon shines, defying skies.
Through driving rain and thunder's might,
It stands unwavering, a steady light.

Lost sailors heed its guiding beam,
Clinging to hope, the fragile dream.
For in the storm, there's strength to find,
A lighthouse calls, uplifting minds.

Cascades of Sweetness

In gardens lush where blossoms play,
Honey drips from petals, a sweet ballet.
Nature hums a gentle tune,
In the warmth of the golden afternoon.

Fruit-laden branches bend and sway,
Each bite a burst of summer's play.
Cascades of sweetness fill the air,
Inviting all to linger there.

The Ultraviolet Glow

In twilight's hush, the colors blend,
A dance of hues that never end.
Beneath the stars, in shadows cast,
We find a light that holds us fast.

With every flicker, dreams ignite,
An ultraviolet glow in the night.
Through swirling mists, our spirits soar,
Together we wander, forevermore.

Canvas of Dreams

On a canvas wide and bright,
Colors dance in morning light.
Whispers of a secret song,
Inspiration flows along.

Brushstrokes soft with tender grace,
Stories etched in every space.
Visions bloom like flowers rare,
Held within the artist's care.

Mountains rise and rivers flow,
Every hue begins to glow.
Dreams take flight, unbound, and free,
In this world of fantasy.

A palette rich with hopes and fears,
Capturing laughter, joy, and tears.
In this realm of endless themes,
Life unfolds in vibrant dreams.

When the canvas starts to speak,
Words unspoken, strong yet meek.
Every shade tells tales of old,
In this art, the heart is bold.

The Light Between Us

In shadows deep, a spark ignites,
Two souls dance in tender lights.
Illuminated paths we find,
A bond so strong, yet intertwined.

Your laughter echoes in the night,
Like stars that shine with pure delight.
Each glance we share ignites the flame,
A language sweet, without a name.

Through every storm, we'll stand as one,
Two hearts joined, a race well-run.
Together in a boundless space,
Our love, a glow, a warm embrace.

With every heartbeat, time stands still,
As moments pass, we share the thrill.
In silence, in the whispers low,
The light between us starts to grow.

Hand in hand, we face the dawn,
With every twilight, fears are gone.
Our journey bright, forever true,
In every breath, I see you too.

Unseen Forces

A gentle pull, an unseen thread,
Guiding hearts where dreams are led.
Beyond the veil of time and space,
Mysteries weave a warm embrace.

In twilight's hush, we feel the call,
A whisper soft, uniting all.
With every heartbeat, sparks ignite,
An energy that feels just right.

Though worlds apart, our paths align,
In shadows cast, our souls entwine.
A force unseen, yet oh so bold,
In tales of love forever told.

Through trials faced and mountains climbed,
Connected still, our spirits rhymed.
In secret realms where hopes reside,
Unseen forces hold us side by side.

So let the universe conspire,
To breathe in us a shared desire.
In every moment, let it be,
The magic flows, you and me.

Fusion of Two Hearts

In the silence, our hearts collide,
A beautiful dance, nowhere to hide.
With every breath, we draw so near,
Creating a bond both strong and clear.

Two souls merging, like rivers meet,
In every rhythm, we find our beat.
With hands clasped tight in the night,
Our love ignites, a pure delight.

Through challenges, we find our way,
Guided by love, come what may.
In laughter shared and tears that fall,
Together we can conquer all.

A tapestry of dreams we've spun,
Each thread a story that we've begun.
In this fusion, we'll share our art,
Two lives entwined, one beating heart.

In whispered vows, we pledge our truth,
The fire of love, a living proof.
As journeys blaze and shadows part,
We celebrate the fusion of our hearts.

Soulmates in the Cosmos

In the dance of stars we meet,
Fates entwined in cosmic heat.
Bound by threads of light and dream,
Together, we form a radiant beam.

Galaxies spin in our eyes,
Whispers of love in starlit skies.
Across the void, our spirits soar,
Soulmates forever, forevermore.

Time may bend, but our hearts true,
In every lifetime, I'll find you.
A universe vast, yet so small,
In your arms, I feel it all.

With every comet's fleeting trail,
We rise together, never pale.
In the tapestry of night's embrace,
I see your light, your timeless grace.

Through cosmic storms and gentle tides,
We navigate where love abides.
In this expanse, our voices blend,
Soulmates in the cosmos, no end.

The Symphony of Us

In the quiet, a melody plays,
Notes of love in gentle rays.
With every glance, a harmony starts,
The symphony of intertwined hearts.

Your laughter, like a sweet refrain,
Echoes softly, eases the pain.
In each moment, we find the key,
To unlock what we're meant to be.

Through highs and lows, our song remains,
Music flows through joys and pains.
Together we dance, we leap and twirl,
Melodies of a boy and girl.

With fingertips brushing like strings on a lute,
We compose our story, absolute.
In the wings of the night, we sway,
Creating dreams that never fray.

So let the world fade into mist,
In this symphony, we coexist.
Two souls bound by a timeless trust,
In the shadows, it's just us.

Underneath the Same Sky

Underneath the same vast sky,
Two hearts beat as time goes by.
In quiet moments, we stand still,
Whispered wishes, a shared thrill.

Stars above, our silent guides,
Woven dreams where love abides.
Through storms and sun, we find our way,
Together facing each new day.

Clouds may gather, shadows fall,
Yet in your gaze, I have it all.
As the moonlight bathes the earth,
I see in you my truest worth.

We chase the dawn, a golden hue,
With every dawn, my heart is true.
Underneath the heavens, we belong,
In this embrace, we are strong.

The night may fade, but love will stand,
Hand in hand, we'll weave this strand.
Underneath the ever-turning sky,
Together, forever, you and I.

Forest of Forever

In the heart of the ancient trees,
Whispers dance upon the breeze.
A path unfolds beneath our feet,
In this forest, our souls meet.

Leaves shimmer like emeralds bright,
In their shade, we find our light.
Every step brings us closer still,
In the silence, we share our will.

Roots run deep, a silent vow,
In the moment, here and now.
With the rustling leaves, a secret spoken,
In this haven, love's unbroken.

Through sunlight and shadows we roam,
In this forest, we've made a home.
The world beyond fades away,
In each other's arms, we sway.

As time meanders like a stream,
We become each other's dream.
In the whispers of the trees we trust,
In the forest of forever, it's just us.

Radiance of Togetherness

In the glow of twilight's embrace,
Two hearts dance, a timeless grace.
Laughter weaves through evening's air,
Together they are bold and rare.

Hand in hand, they forge a way,
Bright as stars that light the gray.
With whispered dreams they weave a tale,
In unity, they shall not pale.

Through storms and calm, their spirits soar,
Building bridges, they explore.
In silence shared, their love ignites,
A beacon shining through the nights.

Each moment cherished, love's sweet sound,
In every heartbeat, joy is found.
Like shadows merging, shades of light,
Together, they embrace the night.

Their radiance bright, a constant flame,
In this dance, they'll never wane.
With every dawn, their bond renews,
In togetherness, life's sweetest muse.

Threads of Desire

A tapestry of dreams unfolds,
Woven tightly, passion holds.
Each thread a whisper, bold yet shy,
In the fabric of hearts, they lie.

Desire ignites with every glance,
A silent song, a daring chance.
In the night, their souls entwined,
In this dance, pure love defined.

With every moment, colors blend,
A glorious truth, no need to pretend.
In the warmth of a tender sigh,
Their spirits soar, they learn to fly.

Through the weft and warp of fate,
They find a love, it's never late.
With gentle hands, they pull each strand,
Together, they make a perfect band.

Threads of longing, bright and clear,
Each heartbeat whispers, stay right here.
In the softness of velvet light,
They weave their dreams into the night.

Starlit Promises

Underneath the vast night sky,
Two souls whisper, never shy.
Stars above like diamonds shine,
In their hearts, a love divine.

Promises made in silver light,
Guiding them through the darkest night.
Each vow, a spark that gently glows,
In the silence, their love grows.

Hand in hand, they chase the dawn,
With every step, a bond reborn.
Through cosmic tides, they soar above,
In the universe, they find their love.

Every star a story shared,
Every wish, a heart prepared.
With every dream, they chart their way,
Bound by love, come what may.

Starlit whispers, soft and low,
Through the night, their hearts do glow.
In the shadows, they'll forever stay,
Making promises that light the way.

Journey to the Heart

On paths unseen, they walk as one,
Through fields of gold, beneath the sun.
With every step, their spirits rise,
In gentle whispers, love defies.

Mountains high and rivers wide,
Together, they share the tide.
In laughter's echo, they find the call,
Taking risks, they dare to fall.

With open hearts, they brave the night,
Finding solace in each light.
Through twists and turns, their souls align,
In every heartbeat, they define.

The journey weaves a tale so grand,
In every moment, hand in hand.
Through valleys deep and skies so blue,
Together, they find a love that's true.

In every dawn that greets the day,
Their love, a compass, lights the way.
On this journey, forever they part,
In the sacred space of the heart.

Light in the Shadows

In the dark where fears reside,
A flicker glows, a soft guide.
Whispers of hope, gently call,
Breaking the silence, one and all.

Through the night, a path revealed,
Each step taken, wounds are healed.
Casting doubt into the light,
Fading shadows, taking flight.

A spark ignites within the heart,
From the cold, we won't depart.
Every heartbeat, every breath,
Lifts the spirits, conquers death.

When alone, we find our way,
Hold onto dreams, never sway.
Together, we'll rise and soar,
With the strength we can explore.

After storms, the sun will beam,
In shared moments, we redeem.
Hand in hand, we face the fight,
Finding solace in the light.

Serendipitous Meetings

By chance we meet, a glance, a smile,
In a crowded place, yet still worthwhile.
Stories weave like threads in time,
Creating bonds, sweet and sublime.

Wanderers lost, yet hope in sight,
Our paths entwined in soft twilight.
Laughter shared as hearts align,
A melody, a love divine.

Moments linger, whispering fate,
Two souls dance, it's never late.
Unexpected turns, a joyful chase,
In each other's arms, we find our place.

With every word, a world we build,
Dreams awakened, hearts fulfilled.
Serendipity sings so sweet,
In the chance we dare to meet.

Memories bloom, forever stay,
In hours shared, we find our way.
Every look, a silent song,
In this serendipity, we belong.

Lighthouses of Support

In the fog, a beacon stands tall,
Guiding ships, answering the call.
Through storms and waves, steadfast shine,
In dark times, you're always mine.

Shining light in fear's embrace,
Your warmth brings hope, a gentle grace.
Navigating through life's rough seas,
You anchor me, you bring me peace.

When shadows loom and doubts arise,
You lift my spirit, clear the skies.
In the distance, your light I see,
A lighthouse strong, you're my decree.

Every challenge, side by side,
With you, I have nothing to hide.
In laughter or in moments of plight,
You are my path, my guiding light.

Together we face the rising tide,
In your strength, I find my pride.
With every wave, I understand,
You're my shore, I'm your land.

Waves of Affection

Gentle tides, they ebb and flow,
Carrying whispers, secrets we know.
With every crash against the shore,
Love's soft rhythm, forevermore.

In the splash of the ocean's grace,
We find solace in a warm embrace.
Through peaks and troughs, our hearts unite,
Waves of passion, pure delight.

Every sunrise paints the sea high,
A canvas vast beneath the sky.
In the warmth of rays that we feel,
Our hearts entwined, we begin to heal.

Flowing together, like rivers wide,
In the currents, we take our ride.
No distance too far, no tide too strong,
In waves of affection, we belong.

With each moment, we rise anew,
Ever learning what love can do.
In the ocean's heart, we find our place,
Together forever, in time and space.

Kindred Spirits

In the heart of night, we seek,
Two souls as one, whispers speak.
Through laughter's glow, our shadows blend,
A bond unbroken, till the end.

In silence shared, we find our truth,
The echoes of our vibrant youth.
With hands entwined, we face the storm,
In every change, we stay warm.

Like stars that dance across the sky,
In each other's arms, we learn to fly.
A journey carved in dreams anew,
In every heartbeat, I find you.

Mosaic of Interwoven Lives

Threads of color, bright and bold,
Stories waiting to be told.
In every stitch, a memory gleams,
Woven together, shared dreams.

Fragments of joy, drops of tears,
Captured moments through the years.
A tapestry of laughter, pain,
In every thread, love's sweet refrain.

Paths that cross, in sunlight's grace,
Each encounter, a warm embrace.
Together we rise, together we fall,
In this mosaic, we find it all.

Timeless Reflections

In quiet pools, the worlds collide,
Time stands still, no need to hide.
Reflections dance on surface gleam,
Whispers echo, a timeless dream.

Moments flicker, shadows play,
Guiding us, come what may.
Memories linger like morning mist,
In gentle sighs, they coexist.

Beneath the stars, we lay awake,
Counting wishes that we make.
In every heartbeat, stories weave,
In timeless love, we still believe.

Gazes that Ignite

A glance exchanged, like candle's flame,
In depths of eyes, nothing's the same.
With one swift look, hearts intertwine,
In every spark, a bold design.

Underneath the moon's soft glow,
A silent promise starts to grow.
With every gaze, a story's spun,
Two souls united, now as one.

In fleeting moments, magic's there,
An unspoken word in the air.
Through every stare, the truth invites,
In our connection, love ignites.

Emotions Unleashed

Beneath the surface, feelings swell,
A storm of colors, tales to tell.
Joy dances lightly, shadows wake,
In every heartbeat, choices make.

Whispers linger, echoing loud,
Serenity finds warmth in a crowd.
Passions rise, like waves of fire,
Fueling dreams, igniting desire.

Tears fall softly, like autumn leaves,
Each drop a story, each heart believes.
Happiness twirls, a fleeting glance,
Life's sweet moments, an endless dance.

Blissful Encounters

Two souls collide like stars in flight,
Sharing laughter, glowing bright.
Time stands still in a fleeting gaze,
In this moment, love ablaze.

Gentle whispers, hands entwined,
In every heartbeat, worlds aligned.
Sunset hues kiss the evening sky,
In this space, we learn to fly.

Every smile, a sacred sign,
Filling hearts, our spirits entwine.
Lost in wonders, we breathe anew,
In blissful encounters, just me and you.

Chasing Echoes

Footsteps fade in the twilight glow,
Chasing echoes of long ago.
Memories whisper through the trees,
Carried softly on the breeze.

Faint laughter lingers, sweet and clear,
A haunting melody, drawing near.
In every shadow, stories play,
Chasing echoes, night and day.

Paths converge, like rivers flow,
The heart remembers what we know.
In silent moments, truth unfolds,
Chasing echoes of tales retold.

Vessel of Whispers

A vessel crafted from dreams and sighs,
Holding secrets beneath the skies.
Each gentle wave, a story spun,
In quiet nights, our hearts have won.

Whispers travel on the moonlit tide,
In depths of stillness, truths abide.
Carried forth on currents deep,
In this vessel, our hopes we keep.

Soft moments linger, tender and true,
We navigate this journey, me and you.
In the echoes of silence, love shall rise,
A vessel of whispers, beneath the skies.

Unbreakable Ties

In laughter, we find strength,
A bond that knows no length.
Through storms and through the night,
Our hearts remain in sight.

With every shared embrace,
We carve out our own space.
Through trials and through cheer,
Together, we persevere.

When shadows start to fall,
We answer every call.
In whispers, dreams take flight,
Our souls ignite the light.

With trust as our foundation,
We build our own narration.
In silence, understanding flows,
An unbreakable love grows.

Through journeys vast and wide,
We walk on side by side.
In every fleeting glance,
Our lives create a dance.

Moments Wrapped in Warmth

The sun dips low, a golden hue,
In evening light, just me and you.
A gentle breeze, a soft caress,
Moments like this, we must confess.

With laughter shared beneath the stars,
We forget the world, its hidden scars.
In every heartbeat, time stands still,
Wrapped in warmth, our spirits thrill.

The echoes of the day retreat,
With whispered dreams, our hearts entreat.
In quiet corners, love's glow spark,
Illuminates the calming dark.

Through raindrops soft upon the glass,
We find our joy and help it pass.
In simple things, our lives entwined,
Moments cherished, hearts aligned.

As seasons change and colors fade,
In memories, we have laid.
Each second counts, our love will bloom,
In moments wrapped, we cast away gloom.

Beyond Time's Embrace

In the stillness of the night,
We find each other, hearts alight.
With whispered dreams in starry skies,
Time melts away as love replies.

Across the ages, spirits soar,
In every heartbeat, there's much more.
Moments blend like colors bright,
Beyond time's grasp, we feel the light.

Each glance exchanged, a knowing glance,
In silent words, we weave our dance.
The clock may tick, the world may turn,
But for our love, forever burns.

In echoes of the past we tread,
Where every word and thought is said.
A tapestry of years compiled,
So timeless still, love's endless wild.

Forever bound, our fates align,
Through lifetimes lived, you still are mine.
In every chapter, woven tight,
Beyond time's embrace, we take our flight.

Pillars of Trust

In shadows deep, we stand so tall,
Pillars built that never fall.
With every promise, strong and true,
In unity, we see it through.

Through storms that rage and skies of gray,
Our love, a beacon, lights the way.
In quiet strength, we both believe,
Together, we will not deceive.

With open hearts, we share our fears,
In trust, we find the warmth of years.
Each secret held, a sacred thread,
In honesty, our souls are led.

Though trials come and moments shake,
Our bond withstands, we will not break.
In laughter shared and tears we shed,
Pillars remain where love is fed.

So hand in hand, we journey on,
With trust, our fears are all but gone.
In every heartbeat, love's sweet gust,
We stand together, pillars of trust.

Colors of Connection

In twilight's hue, friendships bloom,
Laughter dances, dispelling gloom.
Each shade unique, yet intertwined,
A vibrant canvas, hearts aligned.

Whispers of joy, through colors shared,
Silent promises, hearts that dared.
With strokes of kindness, love displayed,
In every hue, connections made.

Together we paint, stories unfold,
A palette rich with memories gold.
Through storms and calm, we blend our light,
Colors of connection, pure and bright.

In every sunrise, a new begin,
With every sunset, the warmth within.
Threaded by moments, hand in hand,
Together we stand, united, grand.

So here we linger, in beauty's song,
In colors of connection, we belong.
Through time and space, our spirits soar,
In the artwork of life, forevermore.

Hushed Conversations

In corners dim, secrets are shared,
Whispers softly, a bond declared.
Eyes that glimmer, words that dance,
In quiet moments, a fleeting glance.

Thoughts entwined, like vines they grow,
In stillness deep, emotions flow.
Every silence, a tale to tell,
In hushed conversations, we find our spell.

Beneath the stars, where shadows play,
Every heartbeat recalls yesterday.
In the warmth of night, expectations fade,
In peaceful stillness, connections made.

Laughter bubbles, muffled delight,
In the closeness found, we weave the night.
In gentle tones, our hearts confide,
In hushed conversations, love won't hide.

So here we linger, time stands still,
In unspoken words, a sacred thrill.
With every whisper, our spirits dance,
In hushed conversations, we take the chance.

A Journey Towards Forever

With every step, we chart the course,
Through winding paths, love's gentle force.
Hand in hand, we wander wide,
On this journey, with hearts as guide.

Sunrise breaks, illuminating dreams,
Through valleys low and mountain gleams.
In laughter's echo, we find our way,
Together we chase the dawning day.

Through trials faced, we grow in grace,
With every challenge, we find our place.
In whispered hopes, we rise and fall,
On this journey, we conquer all.

Starlit nights hold memories tight,
In every heartbeat, our souls ignite.
Across the horizon, forever calls,
As love's sweet anthem, in silence, falls.

So here we travel, side by side,
In a journey towards forever, our hearts abide.
With every moment, our bond will thrive,
In the story of us, we come alive.

Sails Catching the Winds of Fate

On the horizon, adventure waits,
With sails unfurled, we navigate fates.
The winds whisper secrets, bold and true,
In the sea of dreams, I sail with you.

Through tempests fierce and waves that crash,
With courage firm, we make our splash.
Together we ride, through storm and sun,
In the journey shared, we've only begun.

Stars above, our guiding light,
In the vastness known, we take flight.
With every gust, our spirits rise,
In sails catching winds, we touch the skies.

Across the waters, freedom sings,
With every heartbeat, hope takes wings.
In the dance of the tides, our hearts embrace,
In the voyage of life, we find our place.

So let the winds carry us far,
In the sails of fate, you are my star.
With love as our compass, we will steer,
Through the sea of time, forever near.

Ripples of Intimacy

In twilight's glow we share a sigh,
Soft whispers float, like dreams they fly,
Your laughter dances in the air,
A gentle bond, beyond compare.

The moments linger, sweet and bright,
Each glance ignites the stars at night,
With every touch, the silence speaks,
The language found in hearts so meek.

We weave our thoughts like threads of gold,
In every story tenderly told,
The ripples echo, hearts entwined,
A sacred space we both can find.

In shadows deep, we find the light,
Together facing the world's vast sight,
Through silent vows, our spirits soar,
An intimate dance we both adore.

As time moves on, like waves at sea,
We are the spark, the reverie,
In every heartbeat, love's refrain,
Our ripples linger, joy and pain.

Hearts Alight.

In the hush of night, our hearts take flight,
With every glance, the shadows ignite,
A flame that dances, wild and free,
Bound by a love that's meant to be.

Your laughter rings like chimes of gold,
A symphony of warmth in the cold,
Each moment shared, a story spun,
Two souls ablaze, forever one.

We write our names upon the sky,
In constellations that never die,
As whispers weave through the serene,
In this vast world, we are a dream.

In the pulse of dreams, we entwine,
Each heartbeat echoing, yours and mine,
Together, we light the darkest night,
A beacon shining, pure and bright.

As dawn approaches, soft and sweet,
The promise lingers in our heartbeat,
With every step, our legacy,
Hearts alight, forever free.

Heartbeats in Harmony

In a quiet room where time stands still,
Our heartbeats echo, an ancient thrill,
With every pulse, the world fades away,
Two souls in rhythm, come what may.

Each laugh a note in a golden song,
A melody where we both belong,
Through ups and downs, the dance we share,
In perfect harmony, a loving pair.

With gentle whispers, seasons flow,
The joy of knowing, love will grow,
In every heartbeat, a promise made,
A symphony of trust that won't fade.

Under the stars, our dreams collide,
In this embrace, forever abide,
The cadence of love, a sweet embrace,
A timeless bond in every space.

With hands entwined, we brave the night,
Through storm and calm, we find our light,
In every heartbeat, our story flows,
Together in harmony, love only knows.

Embrace of Souls

In the quiet moments, we find our peace,
Wrapped in silence, our worries cease,
With every glance, a world unfolds,
In the embrace of souls, love molds.

Your eyes, a compass, guiding me near,
Through whispered secrets, I find no fear,
Each touch a journey, a soft caress,
In this embrace, we find our best.

Together we laugh, together we sigh,
As dreams take flight, like birds in the sky,
In the ebb and flow, we learn and grow,
With the tides of love, we let it show.

Through seasons of life, we stand as one,
With every rising and setting sun,
In the embrace of souls, we ignite,
A bond unbroken, holding tight.

So let the world spin, let the stars align,
In your embrace, the universe is mine,
With every heartbeat, our spirits soar,
In the dance of souls, forevermore.

Surrendered Hearts

In the quiet of the night,
Two souls intertwine.
Whispers softly shared,
In love's sweet design.

Through trials they have walked,
With hands tightly clasped.
Every tear has been fought,
In each other, they bask.

Time flows like a river,
Worn yet strong they stand.
Hearts laid bare and open,
Together, they've planned.

With shadows now lifted,
They embrace the dawn.
Surrendered to the love,
In unity drawn.

Every glance a promise,
Every laugh a song.
In the dance of their hearts,
They know they belong.

Unseen Forces

Stronger than the tides,
Pulling hearts apart.
Invisible currents,
Guide each tender start.

A glance across the room,
Sparks ignite the air.
The unseen force entwined,
In every silent stare.

Whispers of the bygone,
Echo through the night.
The truths left unspoken,
Fuel the quiet fight.

Fates entwined and tangled,
In a dance of chance.
For all the unseen forces,
Lead them to romance.

With every chance encounter,
They feel the pull anew.
Now bound by unseen threads,
Forever, me and you.

Tidal Waves of Emotion

Rising like the ocean,
Waves crash on the shore.
Feelings swell and crash,
Leaving hearts wanting more.

A storm brews within,
The calm before the tide.
Waves of love and longing,
Where secrets try to hide.

As the water recedes,
So do fears and doubts.
In the ebb and flow,
Their love's what life's about.

With every surge embraced,
They come alive once more.
Tidal waves of emotion,
Bursting from the core.

They ride the waves of fate,
With passion's wild embrace.
Nothing can withstand,
Their love's relentless grace.

Moonlit Confessions

Beneath the silver glow,
Hearts start to lay bare.
Under the watchful moon,
Secrets fill the air.

In quiet, stolen moments,
Words dance soft and free.
Each confession made,
Brings them closer, you see.

With every gentle sigh,
They shed another fear.
Moonlit confessions shared,
No judgment, just near.

The night a soft blanket,
Wrapping them in dreams.
Truths whispered to the stars,
Flow like flowing streams.

In the calm of the night,
They find solace and trust.
Building a world together,
In love, they must.

Love's Guiding Compass

In the quiet glow of starlit skies,
We find our path where the heart complies.
With gentle whispers, the winds impart,
A map of dreams drawn from the heart.

Through valleys deep and mountains high,
Love's compass points where we cannot lie.
Hand in hand, we brave the storm,
With every heartbeat, our souls transform.

In the dance of shadows, we dare to tread,
Guided by light wherever we're led.
With every sunset, hope is reborn,
In love's embrace, we are never torn.

Time can wander, and seasons change,
But our connection will never estrange.
Through laughter and tears, we'll find our way,
Our love's compass shall never sway.

So here's to the journey, wild and free,
In the quilt of life, we are the key.
For wherever we roam, we are still one,
Love's guiding compass has just begun.

Fireside Reflections

By the fireside, we share our dreams,
Softly glowing, the warmth redeems.
With stories woven from days gone past,
In each flicker, we hold steadfast.

The crackling wood, a sweet refrain,
Reminds us of joy, laughter, and pain.
Wrapped in blankets, we feel the night,
In flickering flames, our souls ignite.

As shadows dance against the wall,
We find solace in our whispered call.
Each moment cherished, a memory spun,
In the light of the fire, we are one.

Time slips gently through fingers tight,
Yet here we are, in the soft twilight.
With every breath, we breathe in trust,
Fireside reflections become a must.

So let the embers glow and thrive,
In this warmth, we feel alive.
Forever bound, our hearts align,
Fireside memories, pure and divine.

The Tapestry of Us

In threads of gold and colors bright,
We weave a story, our hearts in flight.
Each moment glimmers, a stitch divine,
Creating patterns where stars align.

Through challenges faced, we find our way,
With every knot, our fears allay.
In the fabric of life, we stand side by side,
As we weave our dreams, our hearts take stride.

The tapestry tells of laughter and tears,
Of whispered hopes, of cherished years.
With every thread, memories grow,
In the loom of love, our colors flow.

United in purpose, we craft and bend,
A masterpiece shaped with love to blend.
As seasons change, our fibers shall twist,
In the tapestry of us, love can't be missed.

So here's to the weave, intricate and true,
In every shade, a story anew.
Together forever, with every breath,
The tapestry of us will know no death.

Embracing Destiny

In the quiet dawn of a brand new day,
We step into light, come what may.
With open hearts and arms outstretched,
We embrace the paths that fate has etched.

Through trials faced and mountains climbed,
In every heartbeat, our souls aligned.
With courage sparked and visions clear,
Together we face what we hold dear.

As shadows linger and doubts may call,
We rise together, refusing to fall.
With every moment, we seize the chance,
Embracing destiny, life's sweet dance.

With joyous laughter and tender grace,
We forge forward, our fears we embrace.
In life's grand tapestry, we see the thread,
Each choice we make, a step ahead.

So here's to the journey, wild and free,
In every heartbeat, just you and me.
Under open skies, we lay our claim,
Embracing destiny, we'll play the game.

Boundless Connection

In the quiet of the night,
Hearts are drawn, taking flight.
A whisper shared, soft and clear,
Binding souls, close and near.

Through laughter, tears, and dreams,
Life flows like gentle streams.
Hand in hand, we tread the way,
Together, come what may.

Unseen forces weave the thread,
In every word that's said.
A tapestry of love unfolds,
In moments cherished, stories told.

With every heartbeat in sync,
Time slows down, we start to think.
In a world of endless noise,
We find peace in shared joys.

Boundless connection we create,
In this bond, we navigate.
Together, we shall rise and soar,
In unity, forevermore.

Radiance of Togetherness

Under the glow of the moon,
Two hearts beat in a tune.
The world fades, just we remain,
In love's warm, enduring gain.

Starlight glimmers in your eyes,
A promise wrapped in the skies.
Every moment shared will last,
A cherished echo of the past.

Together we dance, side by side,
In harmony, our hearts abide.
With every step, our spirits blend,
In this glow, we transcend.

Laughter rings like chimes of gold,
Stories of warmth in whispers told.
In each embrace, a spark ignites,
Radiance shines through starry nights.

Through storms and gentle rain,
In every joy, in every pain.
Together, we light the way,
In our hearts, come what may.

Stars Aligned in Unity

When twilight whispers softly low,
A canvas painted with moon's glow.
Stars above, they twinkle bright,
Guiding us through the night.

In quiet moments, dreams take flight,
Holding hopes of love so light.
Across the universe, we connect,
In every glance, souls reflect.

Bound by fate's silent decree,
Two paths merge in harmony.
With every wish upon a star,
We grow closer, no matter how far.

In the silence, truth revealed,
Hearts not merely concealed.
Together, we balance the night,
In unity, we find our light.

The cosmos hums a sweet refrain,
In this dance, we'll never wane.
Stars aligned, our bond so deep,
In love's embrace, forever we'll keep.

Wings of Tenderness

In the heart's gentle embrace,
We find solace, a sacred space.
With each whisper, love takes wing,
A tender song, a sweet offering.

Through storms that threaten to collide,
Together, always side by side.
In quietude, our spirits soar,
Above the chaos, evermore.

The touch of hands ignites a flame,
Illuminating hopes untame.
With every heartbeat, life unfolds,
Wings of tenderness, love beholds.

In laughter shared and breaths combined,
A tapestry of hearts aligned.
In the simplest joys we actively find,
A bond unbroken, gently intertwined.

Together we rise, undeterred,
In each word, our souls conferred.
With wings of love, we conquer fears,
In tenderness, we shed our tears.

Hand in Hand

In the morning light we stand,
With dreams and hopes, heart in hand.
Together we will make our way,
Facing storms and sunny days.

Through laughter's song and silence deep,
Side by side, our secrets keep.
With every step that we embark,
Our journey lights the endless dark.

In the dance of life we sway,
Finding joy in what we play.
Hand in hand, we'll rise and fall,
Yet together we are strong and tall.

Through the trials that we face,
With a smile, we find our place.
In this bond that we have made,
Love's foundation will not fade.

With every heartbeat, every breath,
We cherish life, defy our death.
Hand in hand, forever true,
In every moment, me and you.

Unbreakable Bonds

In the shadows, we unite,
Through thick and thin, we ignite.
A promise made, hearts intertwine,
In laughter's echo, love will shine.

Through trials faced and storms we weather,
In whispered dreams, we draw together.
Each tear we shed, and joy we share,
Unbreakable bonds, beyond compare.

Time may test, but still we stand,
Facing life, hand in hand.
With each setback, we rise anew,
Together facing what's true.

In every heartbeat, every sigh,
A tapestry of you and I.
Through the dark, we hold the light,
In each other, we find our might.

In the tapestry of fate we weave,
A bond so strong, we dare believe.
With laughter and love, we respond,
Together always, unbreakable bond.

Unfolding Journeys

With open hearts, we take our first step,
Through winding roads, secrets kept.
Beyond the hills, new adventures wait,
As we embrace what lies with fate.

In every turn, a lesson learned,
With every page, our passion burned.
Exploring paths, both rough and fine,
In every moment, our souls entwine.

Together we chase the morning sun,
With every heartbeat, we have begun.
In the vastness, we find our place,
Building dreams, the world we face.

Through valleys low and mountains high,
Hand in hand, we'll touch the sky.
With hopes like stars, bright and bold,
Our story unfolds, yet to be told.

Every milestone, a treasure shared,
Through love's embrace, we are prepared.
In this journey, side by side,
Unfolding dreams, our hearts' great guide.

Bridges of Trust

Across the rivers, we build our way,
Connecting hearts, come what may.
With every bridge, we pave the path,
In unity, we find our warmth and wrath.

Through storms of doubt, we will not break,
With faith in each other, we awake.
Brick by brick, our trust will grow,
In every step, the bond will glow.

With laughter's song, we set the pace,
In silence found, we find our grace.
Through every whisper, every glance,
With bridges built, we take our chance.

In the twilight, our shadows blend,
With every story, we will mend.
Trust is the light that guides our way,
In every moment, come what may.

Hand in hand, we'll face the tide,
With bridges strong, we'll always bide.
Through life's tempest, we will stand,
Together forever, trust in hand.

Whispers Beyond Eternity

In the shadows of the night,
Soft echoes drift and sway.
Time stands still, holding tight,
As whispers guide the way.

Dreams blend in the silence,
With each breath, souls connect.
The universe spins in defiance,
As love learns to reflect.

Stars twinkle like secrets,
Beneath the blanket of dark.
Every moment it begets,
Leaves behind a lasting mark.

In the dance of the cosmos,
Two hearts find their decree.
The rhythm of life flows,
An eternal melody.

Holding hands through the night,
Together we will soar.
In whispers, we find light,
Beyond forevermore.

Flames of Devotion

In the heart where love ignites,
A spark unfurls its wings.
Through the dark, a beacon lights,
As passion softly sings.

With every glance, embers glow,
Filling the space between.
Together, we both know,
This flame will always beam.

Fires dance under the stars,
Reflecting dreams anew.
No battle, no lasting scars,
Just a love that rings true.

Through storms and trials we face,
Our bond only grows strong.
In this sacred embrace,
Is where we both belong.

As the winds of fate blow,
Our flames will intertwine.
In devotion's warm flow,
Forever you are mine.

Threads of Affection

Stitched in moments we share,
A tapestry of delight.
Each thread woven with care,
Colors blending so bright.

In laughter, the fabric grows,
Resilience in every seam.
Through the highs and the lows,
We stitch together a dream.

With whispers, we entwine,
Every secret held near.
In your gaze, I find sign,
A thread that conquers fear.

Time may test the design,
But love won't fray or break.
In this pattern, we shine,
With every step we take.

Every stitch tells a tale,
Woven strong and divine.
Together we will sail,
Our love forever entwined.

A Symphony of Hearts

In the quiet of the night,
A melody unfolds.
Each heartbeat takes its flight,
As love's story is told.

Notes of joy fill the air,
Harmony wrapped in dreams.
Together, beyond compare,
We float on fluid streams.

With every rise and fall,
The music binds us tight.
In this dance, we hear the call,
Lit by passion's light.

The world fades to a hum,
Our symphony alive.
As waves of feeling come,
In love we truly thrive.

Forever in this song,
Two spirits play apart.
In the rhythm, we belong,
A timeless work of art.

Blossoms of Intimacy

In secret gardens where roses bloom,
We find the warmth that dispels the gloom.
Petals soft, they brush our skin,
In whispers sweet, our love begins.

Through twilight's glow, we dance and sway,
In fragrant air, we drift away.
The world outside fades from our view,
In this embrace, it's me and you.

With every sigh, our stories blend,
In tender moments, we can transcend.
A bond that grows with every touch,
In the silence, we speak so much.

Hand in hand, we face the night,
Guided by stars, our hearts take flight.
In this space, forever found,
Our love, a melody, profound.

Blossoms fall, we'll hold them tight,
In the twilight, we ignite our light.
This journey shared, a sacred art,
In blossoms of intimacy, we start.

A Haven of Hearts

Nestled close in the evening's glow,
We find our peace, our hearts aglow.
A gentle touch, a knowing glance,
In every beat, we share this chance.

The laughter rings, a joyous sound,
In this haven, love knows no bounds.
Soft whispers float on the evening breeze,
Together we find our moments of ease.

In shadows deep, our dreams take flight,
With hands entwined, we embrace the night.
A canvas painted in hues divine,
In this place, our souls align.

Through trials faced, we stand as one,
In the warmth of love, we've just begun.
A shelter safe, where hearts can thrive,
In this haven, we come alive.

Years may pass, but here we'll stay,
In our haven, come what may.
A sanctuary built from trust,
A haven of hearts; in this, we must.

Dreams Shared in Twilight

In twilight's glow, dreams softly weave,
Each whispered hope, a thread we conceive.
Stars align as the world grows still,
In this magic, we chase our will.

The sky unfolds, a canvas vast,
We paint our dreams, shadows are cast.
With every heartbeat, we draw near,
In this moment, we've conquered fear.

Glimmers of light dance in your eyes,
As the moon rises, our spirits fly.
Together we soar through the night's embrace,
In dreams shared, we find our place.

The nightingale sings a sweet refrain,
Each note a promise that joy will reign.
With you by my side, the stars ignite,
In the tapestry of dreams, we unite.

As dawn awaits, and shadows retreat,
We hold onto dreams, our hearts beat sweet.
In the depth of twilight, love's allure,
In dreams shared, our souls are pure.

The Whispering Universe

In the stillness, secrets unfold,
The universe whispers tales of old.
Stars twinkle softly, a cosmic dance,
In every shimmer, a fleeting chance.

Galaxies swirl in endless flight,
Each moment captured in the night.
Together we wander through space and time,
In the whispering universe, we find our rhyme.

With hearts attuned to the cosmic song,
In this vast expanse, we both belong.
The moonlight guides us, tender and bright,
In this communion, our spirits take flight.

As constellations weave through the dark,
We follow the path, igniting a spark.
In every heartbeat, the cosmos calls,
A love that echoes through the celestial halls.

Together we dream, under starlit skies,
In the tapestry woven, our destiny lies.
In the whispering universe, we find our way,
As love transcends, come what may.

Bound by Invisible Strings

In silence we connect, though far apart,
The threads of fate entwine our heart.
Invisible strings that pull us near,
A whisper of love, always clear.

Through every storm, we find our way,
Navigating life, come what may.
The bond unbroken, steadfast and true,
A dance of souls in skies so blue.

We share a language, soft and bright,
In dreams we wander, through day and night.
Together in spirit, though miles away,
Stronger together, come what may.

The world may try to tear apart,
But nothing can change a woven heart.
Through trials faced, we rise and sing,
Forever bound by invisible string.

Each moment shared, a treasure divine,
Your heart is forever stitched to mine.
In every heartbeat, in every sigh,
Together we soar, like birds in the sky.

Echoes of Unspoken Bonds

In quiet moments, our eyes collide,
Words unspoken, but feelings can't hide.
A glance exchanged, a gentle sigh,
In the silence, our spirits fly.

Hands brushed lightly, a spark ignites,
In the darkness, our souls take flight.
These echoes linger, a haunting tune,
Two hearts entwined beneath the moon.

Through crowded rooms, your presence calls,
A magnet pulling, as silence falls.
In every heartbeat, in every glance,
We dance to the rhythm of a secret chance.

The world may chatter, but all I hear,
Is the soft whisper of you being near.
Unspoken words hang in the air,
A tapestry woven, a bond so rare.

With every moment of shared delight,
An echo lingers, day turns to night.
Though silence prevails, our hearts know best,
In unspoken bonds, we find our rest.

Chasing Rainbows of Emotion

In the distance, colors burst and bloom,
Chasing rainbows, dispelling the gloom.
Each hue a feeling, vibrant and bright,
Painting our journey, guiding the light.

Through valleys deep, we climb with grace,
In every adventure, a warm embrace.
Splash of red for love, blue for the calm,
Each step together, a soothing balm.

Golden rays dance on the edge of dreams,
Carving our path through life's flowing streams.
With every moment, emotions ignite,
Chasing the rainbows, we hold on tight.

In laughter and tears, the spectrum grows,
Each shade a memory, each color flows.
Together we wander this vibrant land,
Hand in hand, forever we stand.

As storms may gather, and shadows creep,
We'll find the rainbows, in memories deep.
With hearts wide open to every new view,
Chasing rainbows of emotion, just me and you.

The Dance of Two Spirits

In twilight's glow, where shadows blend,
Two spirits meet, as soft winds send.
A dance begins, so light and free,
In the rhythm of hearts, we find harmony.

Step by step, we move as one,
Under the stars, our journey begun.
In every twirl, in every sway,
Our souls unite, come what may.

Whispers of laughter, echoes of grace,
In this ballad, we find our place.
Through trials faced in life's embrace,
Together we flourish, a sacred space.

With every heartbeat, a melody plays,
A timeless song that never decays.
In the dance of two, forever entwined,
Love knows no boundaries, only the divine.

As seasons change and time moves on,
The dance continues, forever drawn.
In the stillness, in the vibrant spree,
We are two spirits, forever free.

Eternal Embrace

In the stillness of the night,
Two souls find their way,
Fingers intertwined tight,
In love's warm ballet.

Stars twinkle like eyes,
Whispering secrets above,
Wrapped in sweet sighs,
They dance in pure love.

Time stands still for them,
Moments drift like clouds,
In a world of zen,
Their bond unbowed.

Through trials they walk,
Each step hand in hand,
In silence they talk,
Together they stand.

Forever they'll stay,
With hearts open wide,
In love's gentle sway,
Their eternal guide.

Whispers of Devotion

In the dusk of twilight,
A soft breeze does flow,
Carrying sweet light,
A love we both know.

Promises linger low,
Like shadows in the trees,
Each word starts to glow,
In whispers on the breeze.

Through valleys of doubt,
We learn to be strong,
Holding hearts without,
Singing our own song.

With every heartbeat shared,
A melody is spun,
In all that we've dared,
Two souls beat as one.

Forever in this dance,
We twirl through the night,
In love's sweet romance,
Together, our light.

Unfathomable Flame

In the depths of the dark,
A fire begins to glow,
Igniting the spark,
Of passion we both know.

A blaze that won't wane,
Through storms we will fight,
Burning through the pain,
A beacon of light.

The heat of desire,
Keeps coals kept aglow,
Fueling our higher
Love's ardent flow.

With each kiss we share,
The warmth starts to grow,
In this love affair,
Unfathomable, so.

Through the ashes of time,
We'll rise and we'll climb,
In rhythms sublime,
Your heart next to mine.

Ties that Bind

On the road we have tread,
With colors so bright,
Each thread we have spread,
In the tapestry's light.

With laughter and tears,
Our stories entwined,
Against all our fears,
A bond that we find.

The moments we share,
Are stitches of gold,
In fabric of care,
Together we're bold.

Though distance may loom,
Our hearts beat as one,
In every dark room,
Hope shines like the sun.

In life's shifting sands,
The ties will remain,
With love in our hands,
Our journey's the gain.

Wings of Affection

In the gentle breeze we sail,
With whispers soft, like a tale.
Each flutter speaks, love's sweet song,
Together where our hearts belong.

Beneath the stars, our dreams take flight,
In silence shared, we find the light.
With every beat, our spirits soar,
United souls, forevermore.

Through clouds of doubt, we glide with grace,
In every smile, our warm embrace.
With every pause, the moments blend,
In laughter's dance, we never end.

In twilight hues, our shadows merge,
A bond so pure, a sacred urge.
With every glance, the spark ignites,
In love's embrace, we reach new heights.

As dawn awakens, skies unfold,
Our story writes, in strokes of gold.
On wings of affection, we ascend,
Together, love, our journey bends.

Hearts in Harmony

In every note, a gentle sigh,
Where melody meets the open sky.
Two hearts beat to a timeless tune,
In perfect sync, beneath the moon.

With every rhythm, secrets share,
In quiet whispers, tender care.
We dance to echoes of the past,
In harmony, our futures cast.

Through trials faced, in unison,
Each step taken, a shared vision.
With hands entwined, we brave the storm,
In every challenge, love keeps warm.

When shadows loom, we stand as one,
With softest light, like morning sun.
In veneration, our souls align,
In hearts in harmony, we shine.

In every prayer, we find our way,
A love so strong, it will not sway.
With faith as strong as ocean's tide,
Hearts in harmony, forever tied.

Boundless Connection

Across the miles, our spirits sing,
In every smile, the joy you bring.
A thread unseen, yet deeply felt,
In boundless love, our hearts are knelt.

With whispered dreams, we bridge the space,
In memories shared, we find our place.
Through laughter's grace, a bond so rare,
In every moment, love we share.

Like waves that kiss the sandy shore,
Our souls entwined, forevermore.
Through every challenge, hand in hand,
In boundless connection, we firmly stand.

With every glance, the world stands still,
In softest touch, we feel the thrill.
In timeless dance, our spirits flow,
Together, love, we endlessly grow.

In dreams we weave, a vibrant thread,
In every heartbeat, love is spread.
In boundless connection, we reside,
A journey rich, with hearts as guide.

Symphonic Souls

In twilight's glow, our story starts,
Two symphonic souls, intertwined parts.
Through every note, we find our way,
In harmony, we dance and sway.

With gentle chords, emotions rise,
In every glance, the spark replies.
A melody that gently swells,
In symphonic whispers, love compels.

Each heartbeat plays a softer tune,
In moonlit nights, our spirits croon.
Together woven, notes sublime,
In love's embrace, we conquer time.

Through mountains high and valleys deep,
In symphonic dreams, our secrets keep.
With passion's fire, and calm beside,
In this sweet rhythm, we confide.

As echoes fade, our bond remains,
In music's life, love's sweet refrains.
With symphonic souls, forever entwined,
In every heartbeat, love defined.

Timeless Embrace

In a world that spins so fast,
We find a moment, still and vast.
Two souls entwined, in silence glide,
Within each heartbeat, time will bide.

With gentle hands, we mold the night,
In golden hues, a soft delight.
Every glance, a vow we weave,
In this embrace, we both believe.

The stars above, they gleam with grace,
Reflecting love in our embrace.
Lost in whispers, soft and sweet,
In this haven, joy and peace.

Though seasons change and days may flee,
Our bond remains, a tapestry.
With every breath, forever near,
In this embrace, we shed our fears.

Eternal echoes softly call,
In timeless love, we stand tall.
Together here, we carve our fate,
In every moment, never late.

Whispered Promises

Underneath the moonlit sky,
We share our dreams, just you and I.
Words like petals, softly fall,
In whispered tones, we heed the call.

Promises, like threads they weave,
Binding hearts that dare believe.
In tender moments, truths unfold,
A story of love, pure and bold.

Every sigh, a gentle plea,
In this dance of you and me.
Through quiet nights, we vow and trust,
In whispered promises, we must.

The world around may shift and sway,
Yet here we stand, come what may.
With every heartbeat, stronger still,
In whispered love, we learn to feel.

A world of chaos, we create,
Within our hearts, a sacred state.
Together always, side by side,
In whispered promises, we confide.

Companions in Solitude

In quiet corners, shadows blend,
Two souls discover, gracefully bend.
With silent laughter, hearts unite,
Companions found in the quiet night.

Through whispered thoughts, we navigate,
Each solitude, our special fate.
In the stillness, we forge our song,
Together here, where we belong.

With every pause, a world unfolds,
Stories shared, like treasures told.
In solitude, we come alive,
In mutual silence, we both thrive.

With coffee cups and books in hand,
We explore the wonders of this land.
In every glance, a knowing smile,
Companions found, all the while.

In gentle moments, we retreat,
Finding peace where heartbeats meet.
Through life's journey, side by side,
In this solitude, we confide.

Serendipity's Touch

Through winding paths and chance encounters,
We find the spark that life empowers.
In unexpected turns, we see,
Serendipity, wild and free.

Every glance holds stories deep,
In laughter shared, our secrets leap.
With every moment, fate entwines,
In the dance of hearts, love shines.

When paths align, the world stands still,
With every heartbeat, we feel the thrill.
In whispered winds, good fortune calls,
Serendipity's magic enthralls.

Through crowded streets and silent nights,
Love illuminates the darkest sights.
In fleeting moments, magic grows,
In serendipity, the heart knows.

Together we laugh, together we dream,
In this journey, we're a team.
With open hearts, let fate unroll,
In serendipity, we find our soul.

Earthy Roots of Affection

In soil we plant our dreams so deep,
Beneath the stars, our love we keep.
The whispers of the winds so sweet,
In nature's arms, our hearts do meet.

Through seasons change, our bond will grow,
With every rain, our love will flow.
We harvest joy from roots of care,
Together always, a perfect pair.

Upon the mountains, we trace our path,
In sunlit fields, we share our laugh.
With every touch, the earth does sigh,
Our spirits dance beneath the sky.

In twilight's glow, our shadows blend,
A testament that love won't end.
Through ages past, our stories weave,
In nature's heart, we won't deceive.

Forever planted, we stand so true,
With earthy roots, I cling to you.
A bond that flourishes, pure and bright,
In every dawn, you are my light.

Bridges Built on Kindness

With every smile, a bridge we lay,
A pathway brightening each day.
Hands intertwined, we walk as one,
In kindness' glow, our hearts have won.

Through storms we rise, on faith we stand,
Together strong, we'll break the sand.
With gentle words, we mend the rift,
In every moment, we share the gift.

Across the rivers, a bond so wide,
With kindness guiding us like a tide.
No wall too high, no gap too vast,
In love and care, our shadows cast.

Every step taken, each voice we share,
Together forging a loving care.
Through open hearts and listening ears,
We build our bridge that calms all fears.

In unity, we dance and sing,
With love's embrace, we find our wing.
With every touch, we spark a flame,
Together, dear, we'll make our name.

Celestial Merging

In the quiet night, two stars align,
Their gentle glow, your hand in mine.
We drift on dreams, so vast, so clear,
In cosmic dance, we draw you near.

The moonlight whispers soft and low,
In silver trails, our love will flow.
Connecting worlds, our spirits soar,
In every heartbeat, I want you more.

Like constellations bright above,
In every twinkle, shines our love.
Together we chart this endless flight,
In astral realms, we find our light.

Through galaxies, our laughter spreads,
In orbit close, where hope embeds.
A universe built on shared desire,
In silent warmth, we ignite the fire.

With every glance, the heavens sigh,
As two bright souls learn how to fly.
In the tapestry of night so grand,
We're bound forever, hand in hand.

Melodies of Togetherness

In harmony, our voices blend,
Each note a promise, a heart to mend.
With rhythms soft, we sway and play,
In melodies shared, we find our way.

Through gentle strums and whispers sweet,
Our laughter rings, a joyful beat.
In every chord, a tale we spin,
Together in music, our lives begin.

The sun will rise, the night will fall,
In every song, we stand up tall.
With love's embrace, we play our part,
A symphony crafted from the heart.

As seasons change, our song will grow,
With every verse, we'll let it flow.
United in rhythm, we shall be,
In timeless tunes, just you and me.

So let us dance beneath the stars,
Creating echoes from afar.
In every heartbeat, hear the sound,
In melodies of love, we're forever bound.

The Language of Silence

In the quiet of the night,
Whispers linger in the air,
Secrets held without a sound,
Stillness speaks of deep care.

Eyes that meet, a soft embrace,
No words needed, hearts collide,
In the silence, love finds grace,
Two souls dance, side by side.

Moments shared in gentle sighs,
A touch that tells a thousand tales,
Echoes rest beneath the stars,
Sheltered from the world's travails.

Nature's breath, a calming song,
Each note carries weightless dreams,
In the hush, we belong,
Lost in time, or so it seems.

Words unspoken, yet they flow,
In the silence, hearts awake,
Love's true language, soft and slow,
A bond that nothing can shake.

Resonance of Hearts

Two hearts beat in soft accord,
A rhythm known to just us two,
Melodies from within are stored,
In every glance, a truth rings true.

The music of your laughter bright,
Dances lightly through the air,
In this symphony of light,
Our joys and sorrows we both share.

Through tangled paths, we find our way,
Harmonies woven into fate,
Every moment, a bright array,
Binding us, as we create.

In the stillness, feelings soar,
Words may falter, but love remains,
A resonance we both adore,
Flowing through our hopeful veins.

If the world fades, and silence reigns,
Know our hearts will always hum,
In the quiet, joy sustains,
In unity, we shall overcome.

Harmonies in Stillness

In moments where the chaos ceases,
A gentle peace begins to bloom,
Among the stillness, heart releases,
A melody dispels the gloom.

As candlelight flickers warm and bright,
The shadows dance upon the walls,
Each flicker holds a sacred light,
In silence, love's sweet music calls.

In solitude, our dreams arise,
Crafted softly in the dark,
Each wish transformed into the skies,
A serenade, each cherished spark.

When twilight embraces the day,
And twilight stars begin to gleam,
Our souls entwined, we drift away,
Captured in a shared dream.

A hush, a breath, our spirits sing,
In stillness, harmony shall thrive,
In quiet spaces, hope takes wing,
Together, forever alive.

Veils of Affection

Soft whispers weave a gentle thread,
Through the tapestry of our days,
In every look, unspoken words,
Binding our hearts in tender ways.

Veils of affection cast their light,
A glow that warms the coldest night,
In each embrace, a promise kept,
In love's embrace, the world can't fret.

Beneath the stars, hand in hand,
Promises wrapped in moonlit air,
In this moment, we both stand,
Defying time with love laid bare.

Every heartbeat, a symphony,
Echoing through the night's embrace,
In tenderness, we find the key,
Unlocking realms of hidden grace.

Let the world fade, let silence reign,
In the warmth of your sweet gaze,
In this dance where love is plain,
Together we shall spend our days.

Constellations of Care

In the night, stars brightly shine,
Whispers of love feel divine.
Each twinkle a promise made,
In this bond, hope won't fade.

Guiding us through darkest times,
A tapestry of gentle rhymes.
With every touch, a spark ignites,
Together we reach new heights.

Hands held tight, we find our way,
In the glow of the Milky Way.
Every heartbeat sings a song,
In constellations, we belong.

Through the storms that life may send,
Your love will always be my friend.
In this universe we share,
Life's a journey, never bare.

With every dawn, a canvas bright,
Painting dreams in morning light.
In our hearts, the stars declare,
In this life, we deeply care.

Threads of Fate

Woven paths we intertwine,
In the tapestry, you are mine.
Each decision guides our way,
Threads of fate in bright display.

With every choice, a story spun,
Underneath the shining sun.
Moments fleeting, yet so vast,
Together we will hold them fast.

In the fabric of our dreams,
Nothing ever is what it seems.
Stitches made with love and care,
Patterns only we can share.

Though the world may pull apart,
You are stitched into my heart.
Every journey you support,
Together, our bond won't distort.

In the quiet of the night,
Threads of fate weave pure delight.
Hand in hand, we weave and mend,
Forever my beloved friend.

Dance of Two Hearts

In the stillness, rhythms play,
Two hearts dance, swaying away.
Steps in sync, a perfect flow,
In this moment, love will grow.

Eyes like stars, they intertwine,
Lost in love, the world divine.
With every twirl, we find our place,
In this passionate embrace.

Whispers soft beneath the moon,
Our spirits rise, a gentle tune.
In this dance, time stands still,
Together, we feel the thrill.

With every leap, we touch the sky,
Two hearts soar, we can't deny.
Boundless joy, a perfect art,
Forever, we won't be apart.

As the music fades away,
In each other's arms, we'll stay.
Through life's dance, we'll find our way,
Two hearts in a blissful ballet.

Infinite Resonance

In the echoes of the night,
Love's vibrations feel so right.
Every whisper, soft and clear,
Resonates when you are near.

In this symphony of souls,
Harmonies of love unfold.
Notes that linger in the air,
Bound together, strong and rare.

A melody that knows no end,
In this rhythm, hearts will blend.
With each pulse, our spirits rise,
Underneath the endless skies.

In the dance of time we sway,
Infinite, come what may.
Every heartbeat, every glance,
Creates a world of sweet romance.

From silence springs a gentle song,
In this union, we belong.
Forever echoes through the years,
Infinite love, beyond our fears.

Gentle Currents

Whispers in the water's flow,
Softly guiding where we go.
With each ripple, dreams unfold,
In tranquil moments, stories told.

Leaves drift lightly on the breeze,
Carrying whispers through the trees.
Nature's lullaby sings sweet,
In the currents, life's heartbeat.

Beneath a sky so vast and wide,
The waves embrace, our fears subside.
Lost in thought, we float along,
In gentle currents, we belong.

Stars ignite the evening glow,
Mapping paths where hearts can flow.
In the silence, wisdom found,
In gentle currents, we are bound.

As tides of time begin to sway,
We drift together, come what may.
The journey calls, our spirits sing,
In gentle currents, love takes wing.

Harvest of Compassion

Fields of kindness, seeds of care,
Nurtured hearts, a love laid bare.
Hands that gather, souls entwined,
In the harvest, peace defined.

Crops of hope beneath the sun,
Together, we are never done.
Tears once shed now feed the land,
In love's embrace, we take a stand.

Each small gesture, vast and real,
Sows the strength that helps us heal.
In laughter shared, in burdens lifted,
In every moment, spirits gifted.

As seasons change, we stand as one,
United under moon and sun.
In this garden, beauty grows,
A harvest rich, compassion flows.

With every act of selfless grace,
We craft a world, a sacred space.
Together, let our hearts combine,
In this harvest, love will shine.

Embracing Vulnerability

In the shadows, secrets bloom,
Fears entwined create the room.
With open hearts, we find our way,
In vulnerability, we stay.

Layers peeled, exposing light,
In gentle voices, we ignite.
Trusting tides that ebb and flow,
Awareness, in each moment, grow.

Through the cracks, true strength will shine,
In our rawness, we define.
Moments fragile, yet so real,
With every breath, the power heal.

As we share our tales of woe,
Let connection's warmth bestow.
Embracing flaws that make us whole,
In vulnerability, we console.

Open arms and hearts as one,
Fearless journeys just begun.
In this space, we dare to be,
Embracing vulnerability.

Beyond the Horizon

Waves of wonder, skies of dreams,
Chasing shadows, sunlight beams.
Horizons call with whispers clear,
Beyond the edge, we have no fear.

Mountains rise and valleys fall,
In nature's arms, we hear the call.
With every step, the world unfolds,
In every heartbeat, life beholds.

Oceans vast, with secrets deep,
In silent waters, stories seep.
With every wave that breaks the shore,
A journey waits, forevermore.

Stars above, like guiding eyes,
Illuminate the untold ties.
With each dawn, new paths arise,
Beyond the horizon, hope flies high.

As horizons blend in twilight's hue,
With every breath, we start anew.
Beyond the limits, dreams take flight,
In endless skies, our spirits light.

Radiant Heartstrings

In whispers soft, the heart will sing,
A melody of love takes wing.
With every beat, a story starts,
Weaving dreams through radiant hearts.

Threads of light in evening's glow,
Binding souls with gentle flow.
In laughter shared and tears that part,
We dance along these heartstrings' art.

Moments cherished, shadows cast,
Time holds on, too quick, too fast.
Yet in the silence, love imparts,
A symphony of tender hearts.

Through stormy seas, we sail so free,
The compass of our destiny.
With every storm and every sigh,
Together, we will always try.

So hold my hand, forever near,
In every joy, in every tear.
A radiant bond, there's no divide,
Where heartstrings weave, our souls abide.

Interwoven Destinies

In every thread, a path is spun,
Two destinies, forever one.
With every twist, with every turn,
Our will to love, a flame that burns.

Through winding roads and valleys low,
Together, we embrace the flow.
Hand in hand, we face the tide,
In this great dance, we won't subside.

Bound by dreams and hopes we share,
In every moment, love is rare.
With gentle whispers, hearts will soar,
Interwoven lives forevermore.

As seasons change and stars align,
In every heartbeat, love will shine.
In shallows deep or mountains grand,
We find our strength, we take our stand.

So let us wander, you and I,
Through labyrinths beneath the sky.
In every step, a promise keeps,
In interwoven destinies, love leaps.

The Comfort of Presence

In quiet moments, silence speaks,
The comfort found in gentle tweaks.
A simple touch, a glance so kind,
In your embrace, my peace I find.

Through hardship's maze, together tread,
With whispered hopes, we forge ahead.
In laughter shared and sorrows eased,
Our hearts entwined, forever pleased.

A shared cup warms the chill of night,
In every hug, a source of light.
With every breath, my soul's at ease,
In presence felt, my heart agrees.

Though miles may stretch and time may part,
The comfort lingers in the heart.
In every beat, a promise stays,
In presence felt, love always plays.

So here we stand, in stillness shared,
The world dissolves, our spirits bared.
In every glance, a world anew,
The comfort of presence, me and you.

Where Shadows Meet Light

In twilight's grasp, the shadows dance,
Between the dusk, a fleeting chance.
Where light and dark embrace and play,
A canvas brightening the gray.

These hues of life, both soft and bold,
In stories whispered, truths unfold.
For every shadow tells a tale,
Of journeys taken, winds that sail.

In every heart, a spark remains,
Where shadows meet, love never wanes.
The flicker in the deepest night,
Will guide us home towards the light.

Through trials faced, we learn to see,
The beauty found in you and me.
Together forged in warmth and strife,
Where shadows meet, we find our life.

So let us wander, hand in hand,
In this grand scheme, we will withstand.
Where darkness fades and bright hearts gleam,
In unity, we dare to dream.

Milton Keynes UK
Ingram Content Group UK Ltd.
UKHW022224251124
451566UK00006B/125

9 789916 896310